Animals

Nature's
RECORD-BREAKERS

Animals

Written by Joyce E. Newson

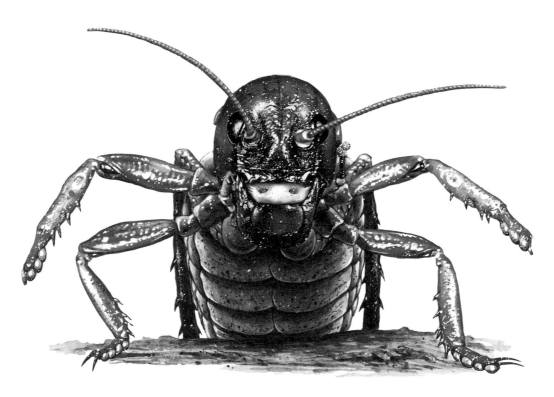

Illustrated by Antonella Pastorelli, Matteo Chesi,
Fiammetta Dogi, Ivan Stalio, Thomas Troyer,
and Susanna Addariao

Gareth Stevens Publishing
A WORLD ALMANAC EDUCATION GROUP COMPANY

For a free color catalog describing Gareth Stevens' list of high-quality books and multimedia programs, call 1-800-542-2595 (USA) or 1-800-461-9120 (Canada). Gareth Stevens Publishing's Fax: (414) 332-3567.

Gareth Stevens Publishing would like to thank Jan Rafert of the Milwaukee County Zoo, Milwaukee, Wisconsin, for his kind and professional help with the information in this book.

Library of Congress Cataloging-in-Publication Data

Newson, Joyce E.
    Animals / by Joyce E. Newson ; illustrated by Antonella Pastorelli ... [et al.].
      p. cm. -- (Nature's record-breakers)
    Includes bibliographical references and index.
    Summary: Provides unusual facts about various mammals, birds, reptiles, amphibians, fish, insects, and arachnids, and includes information about both endangered and extinct species.
    ISBN 0-8368-2473-3 (lib. bdg.)
    1. Animals--Miscellanea--Juvenile literature. [1. Animals--Miscellanea.]
I. Pastorelli, Antonella, ill. II. Title. III. Series.
QL49 .N48 2000
590--dc21   99-026878

This edition first published in 2000 by
Gareth Stevens Publishing
A World Almanac Education Group Company
330 West Olive Street, Suite 100
Milwaukee, Wisconsin 53212 USA

Original © 1998 by McRae Books Srl. First published in 1998 as *Animals,* with the series title *Blockbusters!,* by McRae Books Srl., via de' Rustici 5, Florence, Italy. This edition © 2000 by Gareth Stevens, Inc. Additional end matter © 2000 by Gareth Stevens, Inc.

Translated from Italian by Anne McRae
Designer: Marco Nardi
Layout: Ornello Fassio and Adriano Nardi
Gareth Stevens editors: Monica Rausch and Amy Bauman
Gareth Stevens designer: Joel Bucaro

Printed in the United States of America

1 2 3 4 5 6 7 8 9 04 03 02 01 00

Contents

Words that appear in the glossary are printed in **boldface** type
the first time they occur in the text.

Q. WHAT MAKES **MAMMALS** DIFFERENT FROM OTHER ANIMALS?

A. All mammals are warm-blooded, and all mammals feed milk to their young. Most mammals give birth to live young instead of laying eggs. Only two kinds of mammals lay eggs — the platypus and the echidna.

Q. HOW MANY **SPECIES** OF MAMMALS ARE THERE?

A. About four thousand species of mammals exist.

Q. WHICH IS THE MOST COMMON MAMMAL?

A. The human being is the most common mammal.

➤ Sloths are the slowest mammals. The three-toed sloth of tropical South America moves about 7 feet (2 meters) per minute.

▼ The elephant is the largest and heaviest land animal. Adult African males stand about 10.5 feet (3.2 m) tall at the shoulder and weigh about 6.3 tons (5.7 metric tons). Asian elephants are slightly smaller.

➤ Bats are the only mammals that can fly. The bumblebee bat is the smallest mammal in the world.

◀ The giraffe is the tallest animal. Adult males can grow 18 feet (5.5 m) tall — taller than any other living land animal. Giraffes also have the longest necks in the world.

Fascinating Facts

• Dogs were probably the first animals to be domesticated, or tamed. They are sometimes called "man's oldest friend."

• The blue whale, a marine mammal, is the world's largest animal. Males can grow 89 feet (27 m) long and weigh 165 tons (150 m tons).

• Mammals called marsupials have pouches on their stomachs in which they keep their babies. Kangaroos and opossums are marsupials.

▼ Cheetahs are the fastest land animals. These big cats can reach speeds of 62 miles (100 kilometers) per hour.

7

Birds

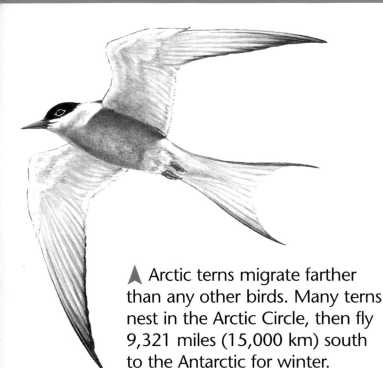

▲ Arctic terns migrate farther than any other birds. Many terns nest in the Arctic Circle, then fly 9,321 miles (15,000 km) south to the Antarctic for winter.

◤ Peregrine falcons are the fastest animals. They reach speeds of 217 miles (350 km) per hour as they swoop down to capture **prey**.

Fascinating Facts

• The wandering albatross has the largest wingspan of any living bird. Adult male wing-spans are about 10 feet (3 m).

• The chicken is the most common domestic bird. About nine million chickens exist in the world today.

• The sooty tern can stay in the air for three to ten years at a time. It eats, sleeps, drinks, and mates while flying.

◀ Pelicans have the longest beaks in the world. Some beaks, or bills, are 18 inches (45 centimeters) long. Pelicans use their bills to scoop fish from the water. A large pouch of skin hangs from the lower half of the bill and holds the catch.

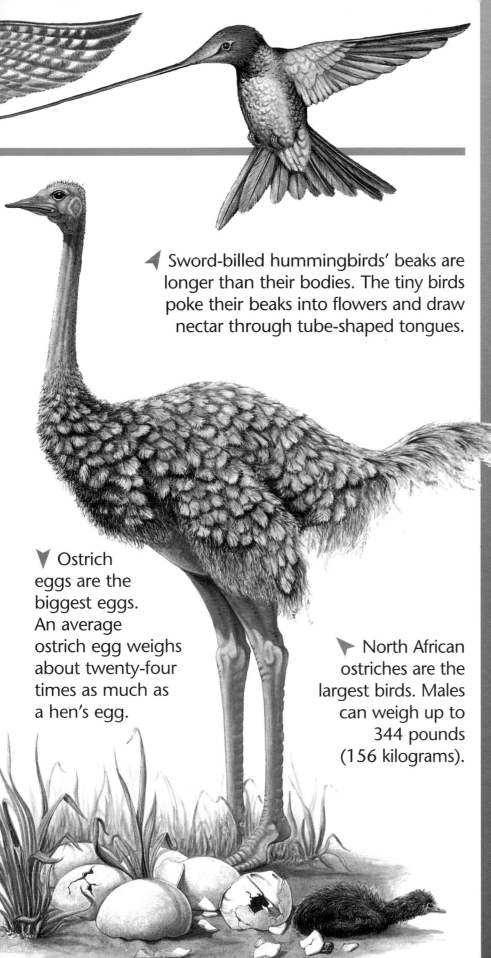

◀ Sword-billed hummingbirds' beaks are longer than their bodies. The tiny birds poke their beaks into flowers and draw nectar through tube-shaped tongues.

▼ Ostrich eggs are the biggest eggs. An average ostrich egg weighs about twenty-four times as much as a hen's egg.

► North African ostriches are the largest birds. Males can weigh up to 344 pounds (156 kilograms).

Did you know?

Q. WHAT MAKES BIRDS DIFFERENT FROM OTHER ANIMALS?

A. Birds are the only animals with feathers.

Q. DO ALL BIRDS LAY EGGS?

A. Yes, but they are not the only animals that do. Insects, fish, and most **reptiles** also lay eggs.

Q. CAN ALL BIRDS FLY?

A. All birds have wings, but not all birds can fly. Ostriches and penguins, for example, have small wings but do not fly.

Q. HOW MANY DIFFERENT TYPES OF BIRDS ARE THERE?

A. Over nine thousand different species of birds exist.

Q. WHERE DO BIRDS LIVE?

A. Birds live in a variety of **habitats** — everywhere from the equator to the North and South poles.

Q. WHAT DOES A TYPICAL REPTILE LOOK LIKE?

A. Tough question! Reptiles are **diverse**-looking animals that have some physical features in common.

Q. DO ALL REPTILES SLITHER ALONG THE GROUND LIKE SNAKES?

A. No. Scientists divide reptiles into four groups: crocodiles, snakes and lizards, turtles, and tuataras. Snakes slither, but the others have legs.

Q. DO THESE REPTILE GROUPS HAVE ANYTHING IN COMMON?

A. Yes. Like fish and **amphibians**, reptiles are all cold-blooded animals, or **ectotherms**.

Q. DO ALL REPTILES LAY EGGS?

A. No. Most reptiles lay eggs. Some species of lizards and snakes, however, keep the eggs inside their bodies until they hatch.

Reptiles

◀ Anacondas are the heaviest snakes. They can weigh up to 518 pounds (235 kg). Anacondas live in swamps near rivers and lakes in South America.

◀ Tuataras are the only surviving members of an entire **order** of reptiles. This order appeared on Earth over 220 million years ago. All of its members, except the tuatara, died out 65 million years ago.

▼ Leatherback turtles are the biggest turtles. They can weigh up to 1,103 pounds (500 kg). They live in seas and oceans around the world.

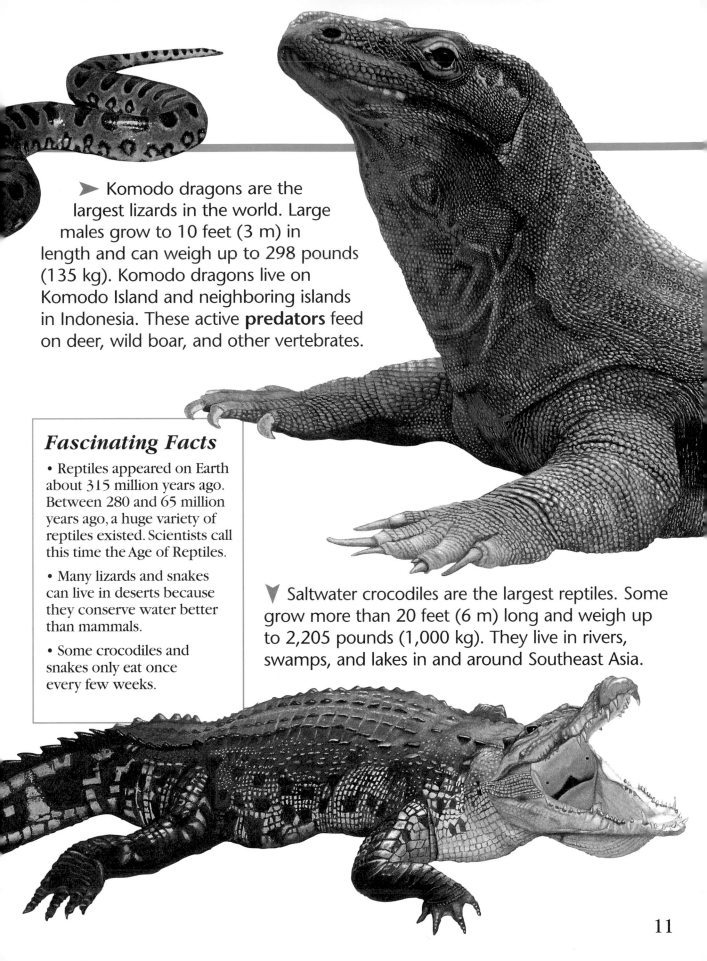

➤ Komodo dragons are the largest lizards in the world. Large males grow to 10 feet (3 m) in length and can weigh up to 298 pounds (135 kg). Komodo dragons live on Komodo Island and neighboring islands in Indonesia. These active **predators** feed on deer, wild boar, and other vertebrates.

Fascinating Facts

• Reptiles appeared on Earth about 315 million years ago. Between 280 and 65 million years ago, a huge variety of reptiles existed. Scientists call this time the Age of Reptiles.

• Many lizards and snakes can live in deserts because they conserve water better than mammals.

• Some crocodiles and snakes only eat once every few weeks.

▼ Saltwater crocodiles are the largest reptiles. Some grow more than 20 feet (6 m) long and weigh up to 2,205 pounds (1,000 kg). They live in rivers, swamps, and lakes in and around Southeast Asia.

Amphibians

◄ Japanese giant salamanders are the biggest amphibians. They can grow over 5 feet (1.5 m) long. These salamanders spend all their lives in water.

▼ Goliath frogs are the largest, heaviest frogs. They can weigh up to 8 pounds (3.5 kg) and measure up to 16 inches (40 cm) in length. Goliath frogs live in western Africa.

Fascinating Facts

• Although different in appearance and lifestyle, frogs and toads both belong to the same group of tailless amphibians.

• In China and Japan, giant salamanders are considered good to eat. People "fish" for them using a rod and line.

• Amphibians were the first vertebrates to live on land. They are the **ancestors** of all reptiles, birds, and mammals.

▲ Olms have no eyes. These newts, or salamanders, live all their lives in the darkness of underground streams. They have eyes at birth, but, since their eyes are never used, they gradually disappear.

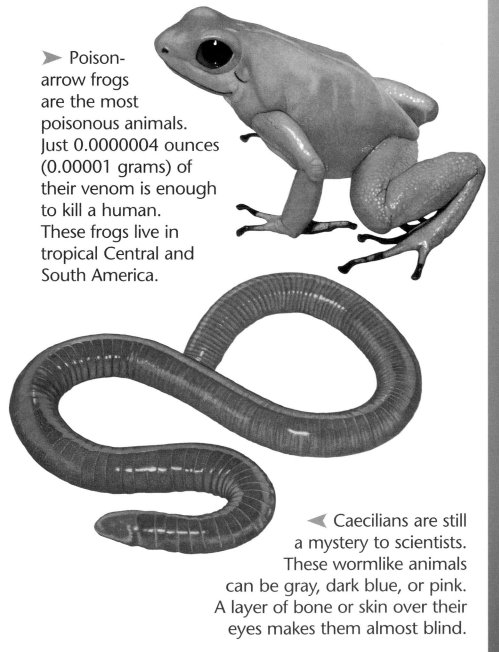

➤ Poison-arrow frogs are the most poisonous animals. Just 0.0000004 ounces (0.00001 grams) of their venom is enough to kill a human. These frogs live in tropical Central and South America.

◄ Caecilians are still a mystery to scientists. These wormlike animals can be gray, dark blue, or pink. A layer of bone or skin over their eyes makes them almost blind.

Did you know?

Q. WHAT DOES THE WORD *AMPHIBIAN* MEAN?

A. *Amphibian* is a Greek word meaning "a being with a double life." Amphibians have a "double life" because they can live both on land and in water.

Q. DO *ALL* AMPHIBIANS LIVE BOTH IN WATER AND ON LAND?

A. No. Most species do, but some species live only in water, while others spend their entire lives on land.

Q. HOW MANY TYPES OF AMPHIBIANS ARE THERE?

A. Amphibians are the smallest **class** of animals. This class includes about four thousand different species. Scientists divide amphibians into three groups: salamanders, frogs, and caecilians.

Q. WHAT DO AMPHIBIANS HAVE IN COMMON?

A. Amphibians are all ectotherms, or cold-blooded animals. They cannot control the temperature of their bodies. They need heat from the sun or another source to keep themselves warm.

Fish

Q. WHAT IS A FISH?

A. The word *fish* is used to describe a variety of aquatic animals, some of which have little in common. Basically, a fish is a vertebrate that lives in water and is not a mammal, a reptile, or an amphibian.

Q. HOW OLD ARE FISH?

A. Fish are the oldest vertebrates. They **evolved** over 500 million years ago. All vertebrates, including humans, are **descendants** of fish.

Q. HOW MANY DIFFERENT TYPES OF FISH ARE THERE?

A. More than twenty thousand species of fish exist. Fish are divided into three groups: hagfishes and lampreys, cartilaginous fish, and bony fish. About 90 percent of fish are bony fish.

◀ Whale sharks are the largest fish. They grow up to 59 feet (18 m) in length and are very **rare**. Whale sharks feed on plankton that they filter from the water.

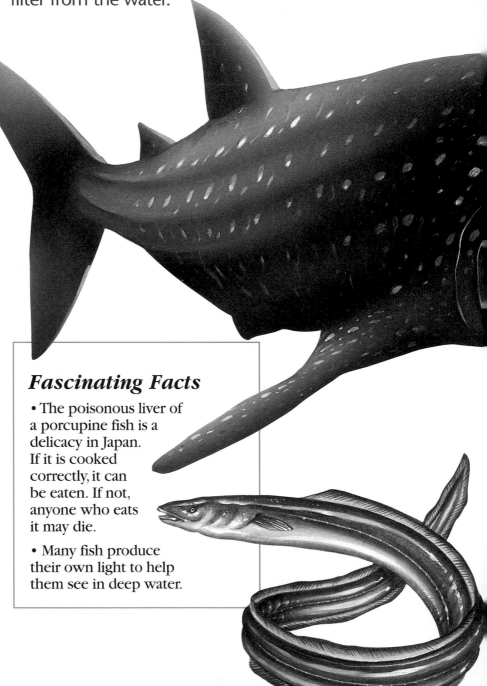

Fascinating Facts

• The poisonous liver of a porcupine fish is a delicacy in Japan. If it is cooked correctly, it can be eaten. If not, anyone who eats it may die.

• Many fish produce their own light to help them see in deep water.

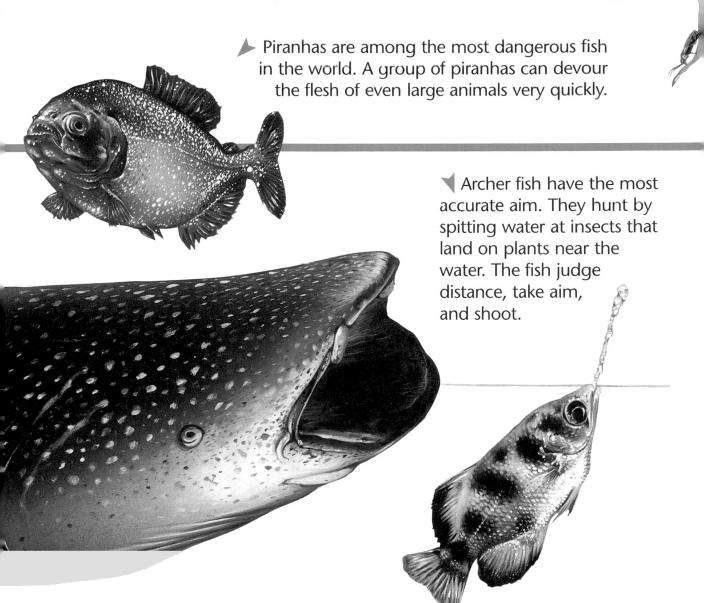

◢ Piranhas are among the most dangerous fish in the world. A group of piranhas can devour the flesh of even large animals very quickly.

◣ Archer fish have the most accurate aim. They hunt by spitting water at insects that land on plants near the water. The fish judge distance, take aim, and shoot.

◤ European eels make the longest journey of any fish. The eels live in rivers in Europe until it is time to mate. They then make a 3,977-mile (6,400-km) journey down the rivers, across the Atlantic Ocean, and to the Sargasso Sea, off the coast of Florida. There they reproduce and die. Their young, called elvers, must swim all the way back to Europe.

◢ Stone fish are the most poisonous fish. On the backbone of each stone fish are thirteen spines, at the base of which lie glands full of venom. The fish's poison is deadly, even to humans. Stone fish live in the tropical waters of Australia and southeastern Asia.

Insects

Q. WHAT DO INSECTS HAVE IN COMMON?

A. All insects have three body sections in common — a head, a thorax, and an abdomen.

Q. WHAT IS THE THORAX?

A. The thorax is the middle section of an insect's body. Three pairs of legs, and often two pairs of wings, are attached to the thorax.

Q. CAN ALL INSECTS FLY?

A. No. Insects fall into two groups: those that are wingless and those that have wings.

Q. HOW MANY SPECIES OF INSECTS EXIST?

A. About two million known insect species exist on Earth today. Many more species have yet to be discovered.

◤ Adult mayflies are insects that do not eat. Some adult mayflies do not even have mouths. They live only for a few hours, during which time they reproduce.

▶ Termites build the tallest houses. These insects live in organized groups. Like bees and ants, they are called "social animals." Termites build nests up to 39 feet (12 m) tall.

◀ Goliath beetles are the heaviest beetles. These beetles live in Africa and are among the largest beetles known. They can grow as large as a man's fist.

16

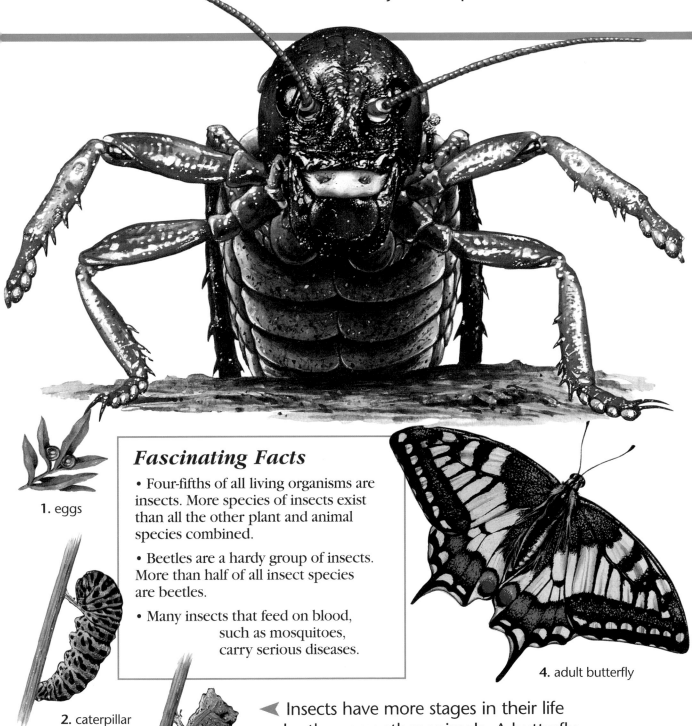

Giant wetas are wingless insects. Ten species of giant wetas live in New Zealand. Some wetas weigh nearly 4 ounces (125 g). These insects did not develop wings because they had no predators in New Zealand.

1. eggs

Fascinating Facts

• Four-fifths of all living organisms are insects. More species of insects exist than all the other plant and animal species combined.

• Beetles are a hardy group of insects. More than half of all insect species are beetles.

• Many insects that feed on blood, such as mosquitoes, carry serious diseases.

4. adult butterfly

2. caterpillar

3. chrysalis

Insects have more stages in their life cycles than any other animals. A butterfly, for example, begins as an egg (1), turns into a caterpillar (2), then into a chrysalis (3), and finally into an adult butterfly (4).

17

Arachnids

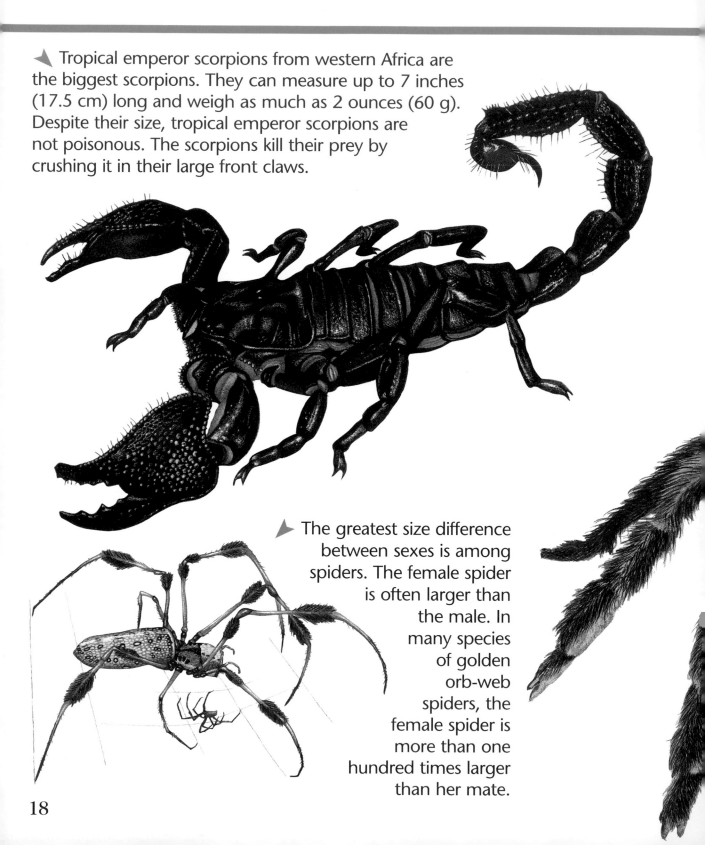

◀ Tropical emperor scorpions from western Africa are the biggest scorpions. They can measure up to 7 inches (17.5 cm) long and weigh as much as 2 ounces (60 g). Despite their size, tropical emperor scorpions are not poisonous. The scorpions kill their prey by crushing it in their large front claws.

▶ The greatest size difference between sexes is among spiders. The female spider is often larger than the male. In many species of golden orb-web spiders, the female spider is more than one hundred times larger than her mate.

18

◀ Ticks and mites are the smallest **arachnids**. They are also the most widespread.

Fascinating Facts

• Some bird-eating spiders in South America hunt and kill small birds, mice, and lizards.

• Ticks and mites are **parasites**. They live off of other animals and plants. Their mouths are adapted for biting and sucking.

• Scorpions were among the first animals to live on land.

▶ Solifughes are the fastest arachnids. Some species of solifughes spend all their time on the move.

▲ South American goliath bird-eating spiders are the largest living spiders. They can grow to almost 11 inches (28 cm) across, including their legs.

Q. WHAT DO TYPICAL ARACHNIDS LOOK LIKE?

A. Most arachnids have four pairs of legs, plus two other pairs of appendages. An arachnid's body is divided into two parts. Spiders, ticks, mites, and scorpions are common arachnids.

Q. WHAT DO ARACHNIDS EAT?

A. Most arachnids are meat-eaters, or carnivores. Many arachnids use poison to kill prey.

Q. WHERE DO ARACHNIDS LIVE?

A. Arachnids are everywhere! They **adapt** to many different **environments**. Some species of arachnids live on every continent on Earth. After insects, arachnids are the second largest group of animals.

Other Invertebrates

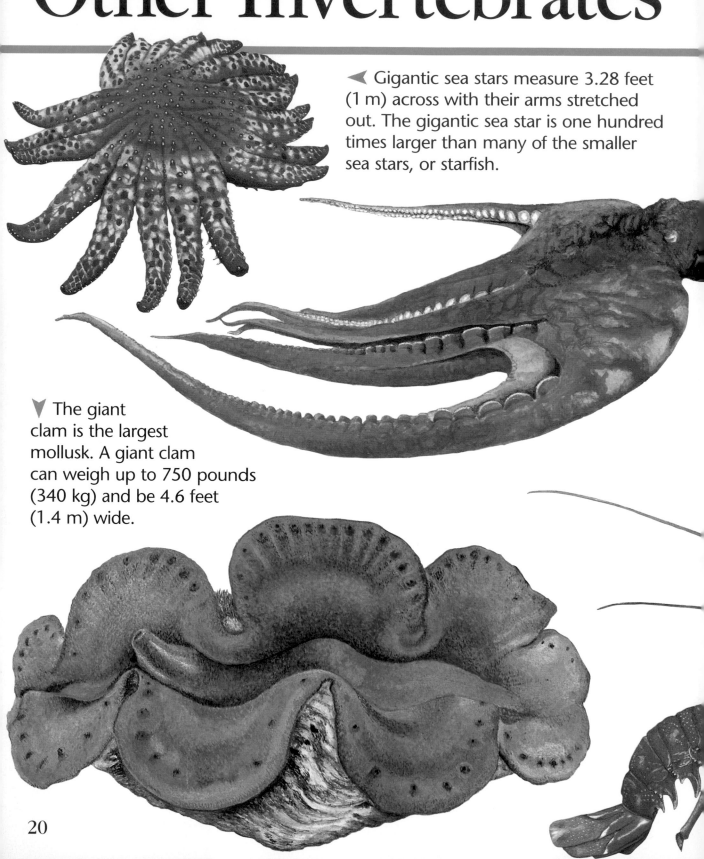

◄ Gigantic sea stars measure 3.28 feet (1 m) across with their arms stretched out. The gigantic sea star is one hundred times larger than many of the smaller sea stars, or starfish.

▼ The giant clam is the largest mollusk. A giant clam can weigh up to 750 pounds (340 kg) and be 4.6 feet (1.4 m) wide.

➤ The Portuguese man-of-war is one of the most dangerous animals in tropical seas. Prey caught in its long, poisonous tentacles are quickly eaten.

Fascinating Fact

Some starfish can grow a new arm if one is damaged or broken. Some starfish can even grow a whole new body from just one arm!

◀ The common octopus is the most intelligent **invertebrate**. It lives in tropical and temperate seas throughout the world.

➤ Slugs and snails are the hungriest **gastropods**. African snails, about 1 foot (30 cm) in length, are some of the hungriest snails. They can sometimes destroy an entire harvest.

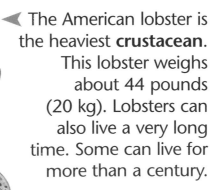

◀ The American lobster is the heaviest **crustacean**. This lobster weighs about 44 pounds (20 kg). Lobsters can also live a very long time. Some can live for more than a century.

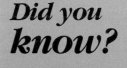
Q. WHAT IS AN INVERTEBRATE?

A. An invertebrate is an animal that has no backbone. This feature is used to separate the animal from those animals that have backbones, such as mammals, fish, birds, reptiles, and amphibians.

Q. WHAT DOES AN INVERTEBRATE LOOK LIKE?

A. Invertebrates are a mixed group of animals. This group includes animals as diverse as insects, coral, spiders, octopuses, jellyfish, and crustaceans. They vary in size, from the tiniest protozoan to the giant squid.

Q. HOW MANY ANIMALS ARE INVERTEBRATES?

A. About 90 percent of all known animal species are invertebrates.

Unique Creatures

◄ Shell-less sea slugs live in seas throughout the world. To protect themselves, some slugs have sharp spikes, and others shoot venom at predators. Some just taste bad!

◄ Sponges are animals that look the most like plants. For a time, scientists thought they *were* plants. Now, the five thousand species of sponges throughout the world are classified as animals.

► The thorny devils of Australia are unique lizards. They are covered with spikes from head to tail. Despite their looks, these lizards are harmless and eat ants and termites.

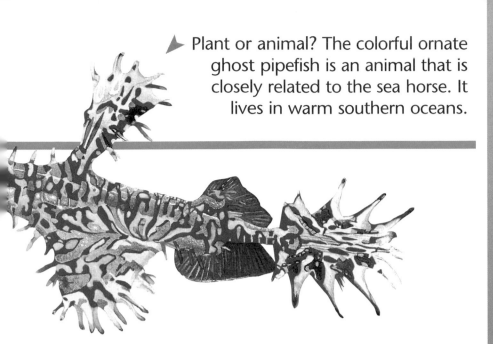

▶ Plant or animal? The colorful ornate ghost pipefish is an animal that is closely related to the sea horse. It lives in warm southern oceans.

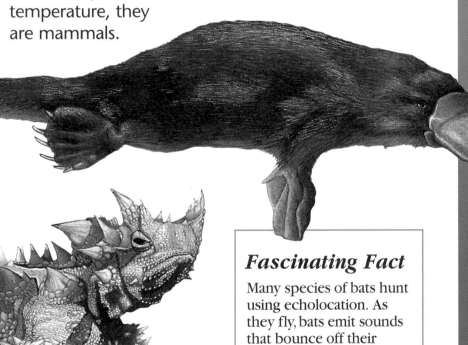

◀ The duck-billed platypus is an egg-laying mammal. Platypuses have bills like birds and skeletons like reptiles. However, since they also have hair, produce milk, and control their body temperature, they are mammals.

Fascinating Fact

Many species of bats hunt using echolocation. As they fly, bats emit sounds that bounce off their surroundings as echoes. The bats listen to the echoes to determine the distance, shape, size and speed of objects and prey around them.

Did you know?

Q. WHY ARE SOME ANIMALS SO STRANGE?

A. No animal is "stranger" than another. Some animals are just less familiar to us. That makes them seem strange.

Q. BUT WHY DO SOME ANIMALS *LOOK* SO STRANGE?

A. Animals may look strange, but their appearance almost always helps them fulfill their basic needs: eating, keeping safe, and breeding.

Q. HOW DOES AN ANIMAL'S APPEARANCE HELP IT?

A. An animal's appearance may help it escape predators. Female birds, for example, often have duller colors than males. This makes the female bird harder for predators to see when the bird is sitting on its eggs. Thorny devils (*lower left*) are covered in thorn shapes to make predators think these lizards are difficult to eat.

Endangered Species

◢ The Arabian oryx is the smallest oryx. It is also the rarest. In 1972, the last wild Arabian oryx was killed. Luckily, a small herd was living in a zoo. They were reintroduced into their natural habitat, and the number of oryx is now growing.

◀ The giant panda is the shyest animal. This rare animal lives in the mountains of central China, where it feeds mainly on bamboo shoots. Giant pandas need a lot of food and spend up to three-quarters of each day eating. As more land is cleared for farming, pandas have a smaller area in which to live. They are in danger of dying out.

The California condor is the largest flying bird in North America. The last wild California condors were caught in 1987 to protect the species. Scientists are breeding them and slowly returning them to the wild.

The golden lion tamarins of Brazil are the rarest monkeys. Only about five hundred tamarins are left in the wild.

Mediterranean monk seals are the rarest seals. These seals are shy creatures, and people frighten them. As people use more and more of the seals' habitat, the seals are dying out.

Q. WHY ARE SO MANY ANIMALS ENDANGERED?

A. Many animals are endangered because people have overhunted them. Also, people sometimes destroy animal habitats by over-farming the land or polluting it, and the animals living there start to die out. Many species of small invertebrates and insects die out before they are even discovered, named, or studied.

Q. ARE HUMANS THE ONLY CAUSE OF ANIMALS BECOMING ENDANGERED OR EXTINCT?

A. No. Some animals become extinct through natural causes. If the environment changes, some animals may no longer be suited to it. This will put them in danger of becoming extinct.

Q. WHERE DO MOST EXTINCTIONS OCCUR?

A. Most animals that become extinct are from a rain forest environment. This is because rain forests are home to more species than any other habitat. Sadly, these forests are being destroyed very quickly.

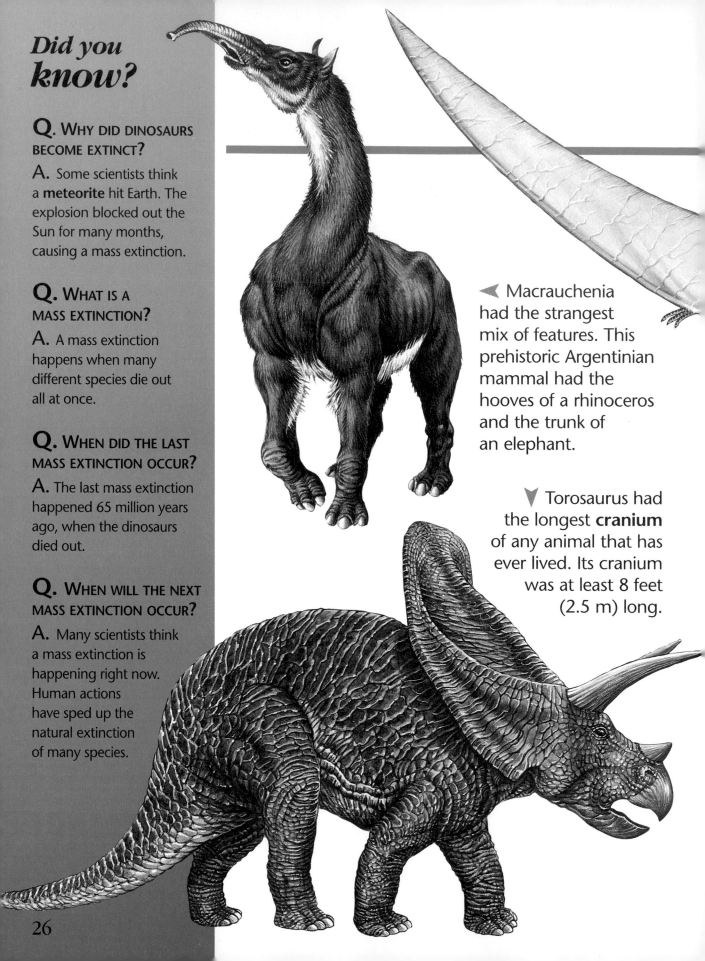

Did you know?

Q. WHY DID DINOSAURS BECOME EXTINCT?

A. Some scientists think a **meteorite** hit Earth. The explosion blocked out the Sun for many months, causing a mass extinction.

Q. WHAT IS A MASS EXTINCTION?

A. A mass extinction happens when many different species die out all at once.

Q. WHEN DID THE LAST MASS EXTINCTION OCCUR?

A. The last mass extinction happened 65 million years ago, when the dinosaurs died out.

Q. WHEN WILL THE NEXT MASS EXTINCTION OCCUR?

A. Many scientists think a mass extinction is happening right now. Human actions have sped up the natural extinction of many species.

◄ Macrauchenia had the strangest mix of features. This prehistoric Argentinian mammal had the hooves of a rhinoceros and the trunk of an elephant.

▼ Torosaurus had the longest **cranium** of any animal that has ever lived. Its cranium was at least 8 feet (2.5 m) long.

Extinct Animals

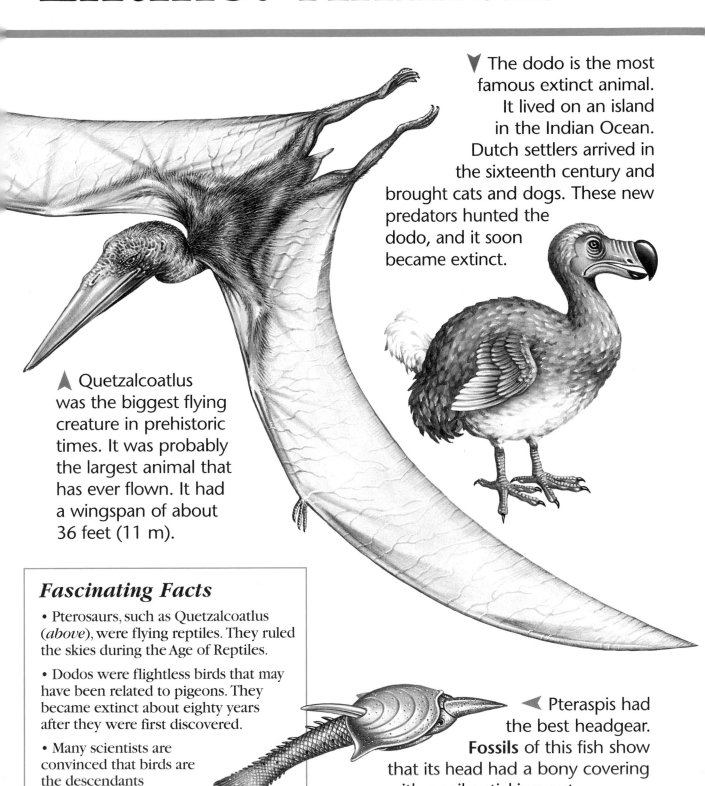

▼ The dodo is the most famous extinct animal. It lived on an island in the Indian Ocean. Dutch settlers arrived in the sixteenth century and brought cats and dogs. These new predators hunted the dodo, and it soon became extinct.

▲ Quetzalcoatlus was the biggest flying creature in prehistoric times. It was probably the largest animal that has ever flown. It had a wingspan of about 36 feet (11 m).

Fascinating Facts

• Pterosaurs, such as Quetzalcoatlus (*above*), were flying reptiles. They ruled the skies during the Age of Reptiles.

• Dodos were flightless birds that may have been related to pigeons. They became extinct about eighty years after they were first discovered.

• Many scientists are convinced that birds are the descendants of dinosaurs.

◄ Pteraspis had the best headgear. **Fossils** of this fish show that its head had a bony covering with a spike sticking out.

More Records

▼ Dormice are the sleepiest animals. They spend about nine months of the year in hibernation.

◀ Howler monkeys are the noisiest animals. Their loud, high-pitched calls can be heard up to 2 miles (3 km) away.

◀ Blue whales are the largest animals in the world. Males can grow up to 89 feet (27 m) long. These whales are about twenty-six times bigger than the largest land animal, the African elephant.

Giant squid have the biggest eyes. The eyes of some species measure up to 16 inches (40 cm) across. Giant squid live in the deepest parts of the ocean. Their large eyes may help them hunt.

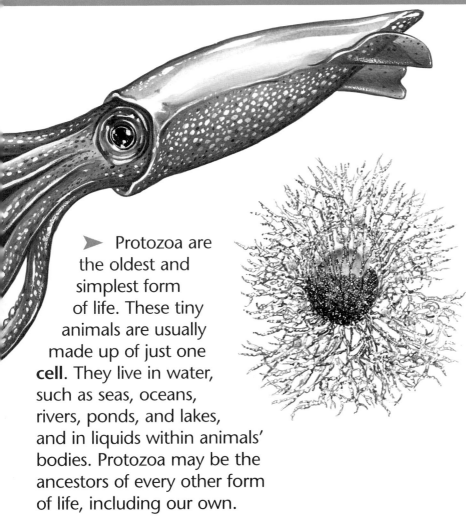

Protozoa are the oldest and simplest form of life. These tiny animals are usually made up of just one **cell**. They live in water, such as seas, oceans, rivers, ponds, and lakes, and in liquids within animals' bodies. Protozoa may be the ancestors of every other form of life, including our own.

Did you know?

Q. WHAT IS THE LARGEST ANIMAL THAT EVER LIVED?

A. Scientists think certain species of plant-eating dinosaurs, called sauropods, may be the largest creatures ever to have lived on Earth. These sauropods lived between 200 and 65 million years ago. Some species grew to about 98 feet (30 m) in length! The smallest dinosaurs were only about the size of a hen.

Q. WHAT DID THE FIRST ANIMALS LOOK LIKE?

A. The first animals were probably single-celled creatures, much like the protozoa that exist today.

Q. WHERE DID THE FIRST ANIMALS LIVE?

A. Scientists believe the first animals lived in water, just like today's protozoa.

Glossary

adapt: to change behaviors in order to survive in a changing environment.

amphibians: cold-blooded animals, such as frogs, that can live on land and in water.

ancestors: people or animals from which another person or animal is descended.

arachnids: animals having a body with two segments and at least four legs. Spiders, ticks, and mites are arachnids.

cell: the smallest part of an organism.

class: the main subdivision of a phylum in the scientific classification system. Frogs, for example, are in the class *Amphibia*, which belongs to the phylum *Chordata*.

cranium: the part of the skull or bone in the head that holds the brain.

crustaceans: animals, such as crabs, that have segmented bodies, a shell, and often pincers.

descendants: living beings that evolved from beings that lived in the past.

diverse: unlike; differing from one another.

ectotherms: animals that cannot control their body temperature. They need heat from the sun or from other sources outside their bodies to keep themselves warm.

endangered: in peril, or danger, of dying out completely, or becoming extinct.

environment: surroundings in which plants, animals, and other organisms live.

evolve: change or develop over time, from one form to another. All living things must evolve in order to survive in a changing environment, or they will become extinct.

extinct: no longer alive, such as when all the animals of one species die out.

fossils: the remains of animals or plants often found in rock.

gastropods: invertebrates that typically have one foot for crawling, a head with eyes and tentacles, and sometimes a shell. Snails and slugs are gastropods.

habitat: the place where a plant or animal naturally lives and grows.

invertebrates: animals without backbones.

mammals: warm-blooded animals that feed their babies on milk and usually give birth to live young.

meteorite: a piece of rock or other matter that falls from outer space and hits Earth.

order: the main subdivision of a class in the scientific classification system. For example, turtles belong to the order *Testudines* in the class *Reptilia*.

parasites: animals that live in or on other animals and eat them to survive.

predators: animals that hunt and kill other animals and eat them.

prey: animals that are hunted and eaten by other animals.

rare: not very many of; not common.

reptiles: cold-blooded animals, such as snakes and lizards, that usually have scaly skin.

species: organisms that are closely related. Members of the same species can breed together.

More Books to Read

1000 Facts About Wild Animals. Moira Butterfield (Kingfisher Books)

African Animals. Caroline Arnold (William Morrow & Company)

Animal Homes: A National Geographic Action Book. Alice Jablonsky and Jeffrey Terreson (National Geographic Society)

Animal Survival (series). Michel Barré (Gareth Stevens)

Animals Are Not Like Us (series). Graham Meadows (Gareth Stevens)

The Extinct Species Collection (series). (Gareth Stevens)

More Games and Giggles: Wild About Animals! Jeanette Ryan Wall and Paul Meisel (Pleasant Company Publications)

Secrets of the Animal World (series). (Gareth Stevens)

Welcome to the World of Animals (series). Diane Swanson (Gareth Stevens)

Wonderful World of Animals (series). Beatrice MacLeod (Gareth Stevens)

Videos

Amazing Animals Video: Animal Records. (Dorling Kindersley)

National Geographic's Hidden World of the Bengal Tiger. (National Geographic)

Wild About Animals Collection. (Madacy Entertainment)

ZooLife with Jack Hanna: Amazing Animals. (Time-Life Video)

Web Sites

About Animals
www.expage.com/page/mrsgindex2

Animal Planet
animal.discovery.com

Weird Animal Express
tqjunior.advanced.org/5801/

Up Close with Animals
tqjunior.advanced.org/5193/ Index.html

KidsCom: Animals of the World
www.kidscom.com/orakc/Games/ Animalgame/

Some web sites stay current longer than others. For additional web sites, use your search engines to locate the following keywords: *amphibians, animals, arachnids, birds, dinosaurs, habitats, insects, mammals, nature, reptiles, wildlife,* and *zoo.*

Index